PRACTICAL

CANVAS EMBROIDERY

Embroidery

Embroidery is the handicraft of decorating fabric or other materials with needle and thread or yarn. Embroidery may also incorporate other materials such as metal strips, pearls, beads, quills, and sequins. An interesting characteristic of embroidery is that the basic techniques or stitches on surviving examples of the earliest patterns —chain stitch, buttonhole or blanket stitch, running stitch, satin stitch, cross stitch—remain the fundamental techniques of hand embroidery today.

In *The Art of Embroidery*, written in 1964 by Marie Schuette and Sigrid Muller-Christensen, they noted the 'striking fact that in the development of embroidery ... there are no changes of materials or techniques which can be felt or interpreted as advances from a primitive to a later, more refined stage. On the other hand, we often find in early works a technical accomplishment and high standard of craftsmanship rarely attained in later times.' Embroidery has been dated to the Warring States period in China (5th-3rd century BC). The process used to tailor, patch, mend and reinforce cloth fostered the development of sewing techniques, and the decorative possibilities of sewing led to the art of embroidery. Embroidery was also a very important art in the Medieval Islamic world. One of the most interesting accounts of the craft has been given by the seventeenth century Turkish traveller, Evliya Çelebi, who called it the 'craft of the two hands.'

Because embroidery was a sign of high social status in Muslim societies, it became a hugely popular art. In cities such as Damascus, Cairo and Istanbul, embroidery was visible on handkerchiefs, uniforms, flags, horse trappings, slippers, sheaths, covers, and even on leather belts; often utilising gold and silver thread. It has since spread to the rest of the world, particularly the UK, where professional workshops and guilds garnered an immense reputation. The output of these workshops, called *Opus Anglicanum* or 'English work', was famous throughout Europe.

Embroidery can be classified according to whether the design is stitched *on top of* or *through* the foundation fabric, and by the relationship of stitch placement to the fabric. Several important classifications include 'free embroidery', where designs are applied without regard to the weave of the underlying fabric (such as traditional Chinese and Japanese embroidery), 'Counted Thread embroidery' where patterns are created by making stitches over a predetermined number of threads in the foundation fabric, and 'Canvas Work', where threads are stitched through a fabric mesh to create a dense pattern that completely covers the foundation fabric. This can be done on almost any fabric; wool, linen and silk have been in use for thousands of years, although today - cotton, ribbons, and organza are frequently utilised.

Whilst there is now a burgeoning market for commercial embroidery, and much contemporary embroidery is stitched with a computer using digital patterns, the art and pleasure of embroidery as a craft is making a comeback. We hope that the reader is inspired by this book to try some of their own!

Eighteenth Century Spanish Needlework Carpet embroidered in Long-Legged Cross-stitch in Wools on Canvas.

In the possession of the Dowager Lady Swaythling.

PRACTICAL
CANVAS EMBROIDERY

A Handbook with Diagrams and
Scale Drawings taken from XVIIth
Century Samplers and other Sources

By

LOUISA F. PESEL

Author of " *Stitches from Old English Embroideries* " " *Stitches from Eastern Embroideries* "
" *Stitches from Western Embroideries* " " *Leaves from my Embroidery Books* "

WITH A PREFACE BY

A. J. B. WACE

Keeper of the Department of Textiles, Victoria and Albert Museum

TO

HER MAJESTY THE QUEEN

THIS BOOK IS DEDICATED

WITH HER MAJESTY'S MOST

GRACIOUS PERMISSION

PREFACE

THE creation of a successful and artistic piece of embroidery demands the harmonious combination of several factors. Though each of them may in itself be of high quality, it may well happen that the embroidery will not be satisfactory because the various factors have not been well combined. For instance, a perfectly good design may be spoilt by a bad choice of colours, by careless technique, or by the selection of the wrong stitches. The first point to be decided is the selection of the design, and this obviously should be suitable for the purpose for which the embroidery is intended. It stands to reason that coverlets, curtains, pillows or chair seats require for the right effect different types of design. Next comes the question of the colouring, and this again should be adapted both to the design and to the purpose for which the finished work is to be used. Closely allied to these is the choice of the materials, which in their turn depend as much on the ultimate purpose of the work as on the design adopted. A reflection of this can be seen in the English embroideries of the early eighteenth century, when silk became more fashionable as an embroidery material. For the seats of chairs and the like a stout linen canvas was employed and the design was worked in wool in tent, Hungarian point, or cross stitch. These materials and stitches can well resist hard wear. For bedspreads or similar objects which would not be likely to be subjected to rough or constant wear, silk embroidery on fine quilted linen or satin was chosen. The last element to be decided before the work is actually begun is the question of the stitch. This point is very important, since the stitch must be well suited to the character of the design and at the same time be calculated to serve the purpose for which the embroidery is intended. Further, if more than one stitch is used, apart from the considerations already mentioned, they should be suited to one another. Tent stitch and cross stitch, for instance, blend well together, and so also do darning stitch and satin stitch. Careful observation will show that in the great majority of cases those embroideries of other days which now stand out as among the finest of their kind owe much of their character to the right use of the stitches. In fact, a detailed analysis on these principles of any really fine piece of old embroidery such as the Dolben Quilt in the Victoria and Albert Museum ought to be of considerable service to students. Lastly comes the actual working of the embroidery, and good technique can only be achieved by practice.

7

The present work is designed by the authoress as a practical aid for embroiderers, especially for those who wish to do canvas work, and since the working of embroidery for use as chair-seats, backs, or cushions is now popular, it should prove most useful. In the seventeenth century the young embroiderers who worked such exquisite samplers, often at a remarkably early age, were guided to a large extent by the pattern books then in use. This book is also a pattern book and displays a varied selection of designs with, in most cases, hints as to the stitch or stitches which would be most effective. Perhaps like the older pattern books of other days this, too, will enjoy the same vogue, and the designs here drawn may be worked and tested on samplers before the worker proceeds to the execution of a piece of embroidery intended for serious use. Probably the best type of sampler to imitate is the long narrow sampler with the patterns worked in horizontal bands in the fashion of the later seventeenth century. In working a sampler of this class after the patterns here illustrated the embroiderer can work the same design in different colours, stitches, and groupings, and so utilize this practice which is essential for the acquisition of good technique, as a stepping-stone towards the choice of colour and stitch when the time comes for the actual work to be begun. Such training, with the aid of the other advice given in this book, should not fail to produce good results and so help towards that revival of embroidery which is desired by all devoted to the art.

A. J. B. WACE.

LONDON,
1929.

8

CONTENTS

9

LIST OF PLATES

10

PLATE.	NO.	DESCRIPTION.	DATE.	BELONGING TO	REPRODUCED IN OR BY
V.	20 21	Powderings from a sampler worked in wools.	..	Miss Beddington.	..
	22	Border from a sampler worked in wools.	..	Miss Beddington.	..
	23	Filling from an English sampler .	First half of seventeenth century	V. & A. M. T.80–1918. Given by F. C. Eles, Esq.	Neg. 48570. V. & A. M. Postcard, V. & A. M. T55.
VI.	24	From an Oriental rug.	..	The Author.	..
	25	Alternative English spray.	..	..	..
	26 27	Filling and border from an oriental rug.	..	Percy Newberry, Esq.	..
VII.	28	Border, found with slight variations on many English samplers.	Seventeenth century	V. & A. M., etc.	..
	29 30 31 32	Narrow carpet borders.	..	..	..
VIII.	33	Powdering in Turkey knot, from English chair.	Middle seventeenth century	V. & A. M. W30–1923	Postcard, W73
	34 35	Two powderings, from a fragment in Turkey knot.	..	V. & A. M. T50–1914	..
IX.	36 37 38 40 42	From an English sampler .	Seventeenth century	J. Jacoby, Esq.	..
	39 41	Narrow borders.	..	..	..
X.	43 44	From a French sampler, by Anne Mazelan.	1745	Mrs. Longman.	Leigh Ashton. Plate IV., in colour.

ACKNOWLEDGMENTS

THANKS.

$\mathbf{M}$Y thanks are due to those who have so kindly allowed me to make the drawings from their embroideries, without which this book would be of little avail.

To the Dowager Lady Swaythling for permission to reproduce her Spanish embroidered carpet as a coloured frontispiece. To the authorities of the Victoria and Albert Museum for leave to make diagrams from their specimens. To Miss Beddington, the late Dr. Glaisher, Mr. J. Jacoby, Sir William Lawrence, Mrs. Longman, Mr. Percy Newberry, Mr. Aymas Phillips, owners of beautiful samplers and carpets

I would like also to add my thanks to my friends, Lady Harvey for her help in checking the letterpress, and to Mr. A. Macdonald for advice in the preparation of the drawings.

FOREWORD

" PRACTICAL CANVAS EMBROIDERY " is the outcome of innumerable inquiries from embroiderers as to design, stitches, and colours suitable for canvas work. It was felt that to publish some designs from the practice of the past, counted out and ready for the beginners to work, would materially aid them, especially those who are far from towns and museums.

My aim is to make it possible for the novice to start embroidery and from the first to make beautiful things. I shall presume she possesses a rudimentary knowledge of needlework, an idea of the necessity for sound craftsmanship, added to the will to achieve good results. I shall give the necessary details in as easy and straightforward a manner as possible. These are the methods I myself would use, and therefore recommend, for that is all one craftswoman can do for another. There are other methods, and if a worker has already become expert on other lines she will be wise to continue to follow them. There are, however, certain underlying principles which occur in and belong to all good craft. Even the expert, if she is keen, is glad to have them summed up by another worker, to see where they agree with her own conclusions. The less experienced embroiderers will find their consideration useful, as it may save some tedious unpicking.

13

INTRODUCTION

NOMENCLATURE. IT is always difficult to find a suitable name for any group of stitches, which will describe all one desires to include and which will, at the same time, make it clear to the uninitiated what ground one intends to cover. Canvas (or cushion) stitches seemed the clearest definition of the group which at this time is arousing interest amongst embroiderers. It is the name which is found in many old books.

MATERIALS. THE *Oxford Dictionary* defines canvas as " strong unbleached cloth of hemp or flax." It is wise to remember this, for it implies a material with substance, a necessary quality in a background that is to be subjected to hard wear. Canvas embroidery is generally used for the covering of seats, chairs, and stools, for carpets or wall-hangings, and in its finer forms, for purses, bags, book covers, and personal articles, all of which require the material to be firm and supple.

As all the stitches are done by the counted thread, a round thread and an open mesh make for ease in working. An open linen, a single hemp canvas, or what is called " Penelope " canvas [two threads each way to the square], are the most usual and convenient types. In old specimens, some of the exposed canvas, where the work has been worn away, looks as if it were a double canvas, as single canvas was generally used ; it is probably only a single one, on which two threads have been taken as the unit for the stitches.

SCALE OF CANVAS. THE scale of the canvas varies, and it should be chosen in accordance with the use to which the work is to be put. Carpets are sometimes as coarse at five or six squares to the inch—eight or ten squares is a medium scale, and twelve squares is found on some of the needlework carpets and on many old chair seats. The canvas is known by the number of threads to an inch, so that twelve squares of " Penelope " would be twenty-four threads to the inch.

WOOLS. MUCH of the best canvas embroidery is done in wools ; but wools with silk for high lights, or silk alone, can also be used. The thickness of the wool, or the number of strands required of a thin wool, depends entirely on the background.

14

STITCHES should be pulled fairly tight, with an even tension, so that the finished work is firm, and the working thread seems then to become one with the background, which should be so well covered that it is not visible. In order to achieve this it is necessary to consider carefully the relation between background, working thread (silk or wool), and the selected stitch, and to regulate them in relation to each other. One, two, three, or even more strands are required if the mesh is large. It is on this apparently elementary matter that the success or failure of the finished work often depends, and it shows the experience of the good worker.

EVEN TENSION AND TEXTURE.

THERE is an endless variety of stitches, on some of the wonderful seventeenth-century samplers, and it has been difficult to make a choice. Finally, I have decided, in this first volume, to give the simplest and best known, with working drawings for their use, reserving the more elaborate and perhaps less well-known canvas stitches for a further volume.

VARIETIES OF STITCH.

It would have been easy to give the illustrations in colour, and they would have looked attractive, but to have done so would have defeated my object on two scores. In the first place, I want this book to be available for all workers ; and it would have been costly to print so many coloured plates and have made the book beyond the purse of many needlewomen. In the second place, so many embroideresses now attempt to work chair-seats, and will, I hope, soon tackle carpets, that if they all copied, most exactly, the coloured plates, we should be overwhelmed, at our exhibitions, with endless articles all much alike. That would be dull —very dull. The idea of this book is to supply hints and suggestions to help the worker, but to leave as much as possible for individual thought and taste, so as to develop originality.

The easiest and most obvious course is to choose one stitch and use it everywhere, throughout the whole piece of work. A more interesting way is to bring in, possibly only here or there, some variety of stitch in order to produce a change of texture, to heighten the interest or effect at some special point in the design. This sounds easy, but it requires skill to make the introduction seem the one and inevitable addition required. It is by such modifications that the intelligent craftswoman can show her individuality, and so make her work just a little different from, and a little better than, the ordinary and more cut-and dried efforts of her less skilled sister. A good worker must think, think, think, all the time, and put something of her own personality into all she does.

MANY of the old seventeenth-century designs are built up on a geometrical basis, and one of the striking points is that often these geometrical designs are so simple. It is the variation in colour and stitch that makes them interesting. They are less uniformly flat than the Victorian Cross stitch, and it is probably also the variety in texture which makes them

SEVENTEENTH-CENTURY DESIGNS.

unexpectedly charming and alive. They look as if the worker had enjoyed doing them and had not been afraid to work them as her fancy urged her. Modifications and variations are not looked upon as crimes ; they are strictly personal, and it is this individual note which is needed in work to-day. If a difficulty occurs, then the worker must surmount it.

COLOUR.

THE question of the colours chosen must necessarily be individual, but a few hints may be of use to the inexperienced and save disappointment over a first effort. Aim at first at keeping the colouring simple, and remember a good effect is more often due to right balance of tone than to variety or brilliant colouring. The most beautiful carpets are often the result of great restraint in the number of colours used, but the colours are placed with such skill that each tells for its full value. Mr. Kendrick, in the carpet catalogue of the Victoria and Albert Museum says : " The beautiful harmony of colour presented by an Oriental carpet is produced, as a rule, with quite a limited number of tones. Red, blue, green, and yellow in a few shades, with black and white, and sometimes violet, are the principal colours." A similar list should be quite long enough for the embroiderer for her carpet or chair-seat. The wording " in a few shades " should be noted. The carpet worker has, for example, several shades of blue, all very near to each other in tone, possibly the result of different batches of dyeing. These would be used as if they were all one colour, and this produces a pleasant variety of tone infinitely more alive in effect than one absolutely flat surface, the result of one shade only.

Just as in writing we are all taught the same letters and use them differently and so produce our personal handwriting, so in embroidery the worker is given stitches, colour, and designs, and it remains with her to use them as seems best to her. It is by selection that she expresses her own individuality, so that her work can really be that of no one else. Colour is perhaps, of the three, the one which is the most distinctive, and it is certainly over colour that it is most easy to come to grief. Study good colour, therefore, whenever the chance occurs.

COLOUR
BALANCE.

A POINT to remember in arranging colour is that it is the proportion and spacing of the big masses of colour that gives the balance to any design. Variations in colour within the main lines (or patches) of colour do not actually tell in the general colour ; they are, however, valuable in giving life and interest to the whole. This they do to an unexpected extent as can be seen in many of the good old carpets.

DIAGRAMS
OF DESIGNS.

THE diagrams are done on the principle of the early samplers. The pattern in outline to give the design, and only portions are filled in to show the shape of the different masses of colour. Where a change of tone is to be made, a line is put within a bigger shape, and this indicates that two or three tones of the same or harmonizing colours are to be used.

FIG. 1.

A Cross stitch or Gros Point. worked over 2 threads single or 1 square Penelope canvas

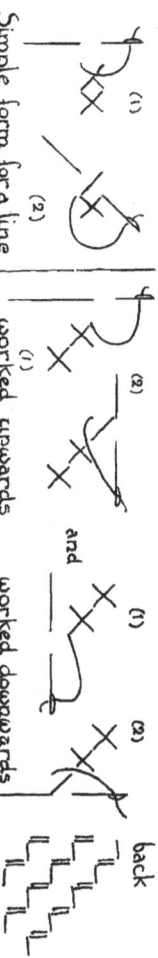

(1) (2)

Simple form for a line.

B Tent stitch or petit point - worked upwards   worked downwards

(1) (2)

back of 1st row

(1)   and   (2)

(1) (2)

back

To descend 2nd row

back of 2 rows.

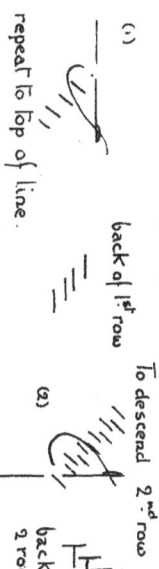

Note. On the front the stitch passes over 1 thread diagonally v ascending, under 2 threads horizontally v descending: vertically. the needle is always put into the gap in the row above.

C 17 century English diagonal cross stitch with a bar - over 2 or 4 threads.

(1) (2) (3)

back of 1st row

back

D Double cross stitch

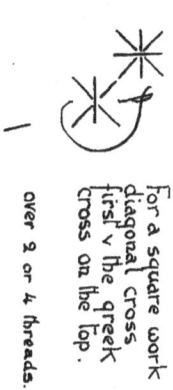

(1)

For a square work diagonal cross first v the greek cross on the top.

over 2 or 4 threads.

(2) (3) (4)

For a diamond work the Greek cross first over 4 threads v then the smaller square over 2 threads.

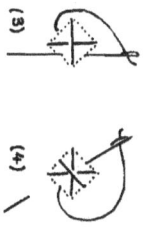

The position of the needle varies for the 4th stitch according to where the next diamond is to be placed.

(Without turning the work go upwards v downwards alternately always working below the previous row. If the work is half turned the direction of the stitch on top will be wrong. Always keep selvedge on the side.

As gros point v petit point are often used together it is wise always to slope the stitch in petit point v the second stitch in gros point v the second stitch direction. From the lower left to upper right hand corner like the S.tb our prevailing wind, is easy to remember.

This stitch is used with English long-legged cross stitch on 17th samplers.
The cross bar is useful as it covers the open space between the greek crosses.

Somewhat similar to N°C with an ordinary cross over the Greek cross instead of the diagonal bar.
When the second cross is smaller it makes a diamond sometimes useful to fill stitch a space.

As crosses in a drawing are so dazzling to count, it seemed clearer to draw the outline of the design only, and the worker can fill in the various spaces with cross-stitch or any stitch she may prefer. To explain No. 14, Plate IV., within the same flower form (A and B), two varieties result by the use of a different spacing and divisions of colour within the same outline. The hatched portions of this design are meant to show that this is the framework of the pattern, and must be worked to tell as such, probably in nigger or some dark colour.

The diagrams can be turned into coloured plates by any worker if she will fill in the colours with crayons. (Blue Bird box of coloured crayons, in cedar ; price 10½d., at Boots'.) In this way it is possible to get an idea of the colour scheme required before beginning the actual embroidery.

DIAGRAMS OF STITCHES.

TO learn the different stitches, it is advisable to take a rough sampler, and to follow the diagram of a particular stitch, stage by stage, then repeat until the stitch is mastered ; and so with each one. In this way they will be found quite simple to understand.

NEEDLEWORK CARPETS.

THESE seem suddenly to have captured the imagination of many workers as an alternative to tufted rugs. They are not really as difficult or as complicated as they appear at first. There have lately been shown, at several exhibitions in London, some most interesting specimens of needlework carpets, and done on similar lines they would be quite feasible for a co-operative effort. One such has just been completed by the Twyford Group of Women's Institutes. The design was taken from a carpet in the Victoria and Albert Museum, and was drawn to scale for them by an art student. It was worked in 2-ply Axminster wool, on " Penelope " natural coloured canvas, seven squares to the inch. Several (three, four, or five) strands of a finer worsted would probably have been easier and pleasanter to work, as the Axminster wool in the hands of some workers was apt to break. The carpet was embroidered by sixty-four workers, and was done in eighteen sections. The joining of the sections was done under the direct superintendence of the two organizers, and did not prove too difficult. The pattern is worked on each section to within four squares of the next section. The edges of the canvas are then placed one over the other and sewn together with cotton, so that the squares lie very accurately one over the other. The pattern is then completed by working over the double canvas. If the work is a big piece it can be hung over the back of a chair and the join worked as if in a frame. All endings off of both ends of wool are best done after it is joined. The extra canvas on the wrong side is then neatly trimmed away, that on the face having been cut close before the final work on the join.

18

FIG. 2.

E) Crossed corners cross stitch. worked over 4 threads single or 2 squares penelope canvas.

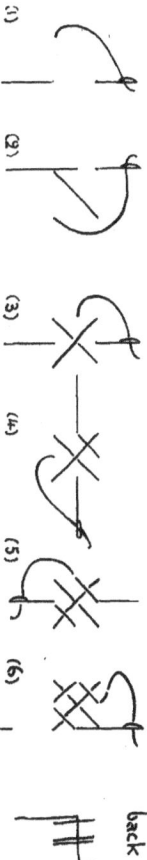

(1) (2) (3) back

(1) (2) (3) (4) (5) (6)

The position of the needle in 6 depends where the next cross is to be placed, alongside or below.
It is best whenever possible to work below rather than above the previous row.

F) Long legged cross stitch (vulgaris or common variety) worked over 2 or 3 threads.

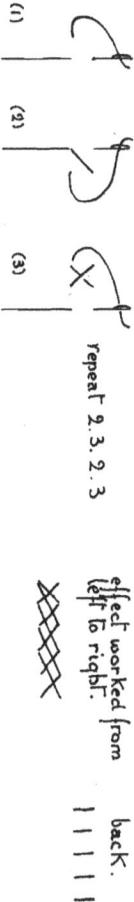

repeat 2. 3. 2. 3

effect worked from left to right. back.

(1) (2) (3) (4) (5) (6)

When this stitch is used as a filling it should be worked from left to right & right to left in alternate rows.
Ordinary herring bone is liked in effect on the right side but on the reverse the stitches are parallel not upright.

G) English 17ᶜ long legged cross stitch with a bar, over 2 or 3 single threads or squares

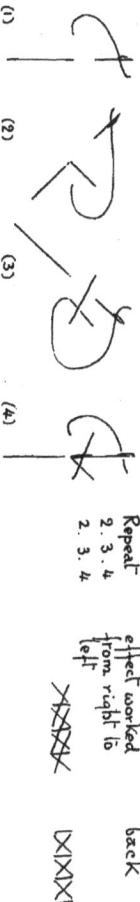

Repeat
2. 3. 4
2. 3. 4

effect worked from right to left

effect worked from right to left

back

(1) (2) (3) (4)

This stitch is common on the 17ᶜ samplers but does not occur in any book of stitches in this simple form.
It can be worked equally well from left to right if it is easier for the travelling to any given point.

H) Single Plaited border or edging - used for a selvedge or turned-back edge -
(1) a straight deep stitch

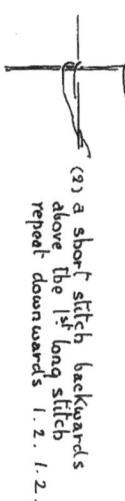

(2) a short stitch backwards above the 1st long stitch repeat downwards 1. 2. 1. 2.

effect

If the second stitch is put through the 1st stitch v not through the material it gives a much closer v more tightly knotted edge.

see also Eastern Samplers Pl 76 A.
This stitch is simple to work if the edge or selvedge is held firmly across the fingers and the stitch is worked down-wards towards the worker

If cross-stitch is used, it is important that all should be crossed in the same direction. Every cross should be completed as it is made, and whenever possible the crosses should be worked on the diagonal, because this gives a stitch with uprights and horizontals on the back, and does not leave points of unbound canvas to be a source of weakness all along the line, an important matter in an article which is to be exposed to hard wear.

The carpet which we have been able to secure for a frontispiece, through the kindness of its owner, the Dowager Lady Swaythling, should be carefully studied, as it is full of suggestions and ideas. It is eighteenth-century Spanish, and is embroidered in long-legged cross-stitch in wools on canvas. The scale is 5 squares to the inch, and it is worked over 3 threads of a single hemp canvas. The centre is a symmetrical floral design, and at each end is flanked by birds, in pairs. All round is a narrow border with a running scroll pattern of foliage. Other designs could be carried out in this manner, and this stitch is one which would not show to any marked extent if it were worked by different workers.

MARGINAL LINES
TO BORDERS
TO CARPETS.

STITCH G, English seventeenth-century long-legged cross-stitch, will be found very useful for lines at the edges of borders, as it covers well. It is wise to use an extra strand of wool to give the necessary thickness. It is easiest to hold the work, with the unworked edge in the hand, and to work the stitch upwards and away from the worker, as this gives a chance of giving a specially firm and regular tension, which raises the line and helps to mark the border lines.

LOUISA F. PESEL.

September 1929.

SOME USEFUL VICTORIA AND ALBERT MUSEUM REFERENCES

1. Panel	.	.	. Dated 1751.	T59–1914.	Neg. 54104.	Is in sampler form, and has good fillings.
2. ,,	.	.		T31–1014.	Neg. 38127.	Suitable for chair. In long-legged cross-stitch.
3. .,	.	.	. Or chair seat.	629–1923. Circulation.	Neg. 56589.	Petit point.
4. ,,	.	.		On loan.	Neg. 57475.	Petit point sprays ; very fine.
5. Sampler	.	.		T80–1918.	Neg. 48570.	Simple powderings and all-over patterns.
6. ,,	.	.	. V. & A. M.	T480–94.	Neg. 45495.	These all three give borders suitable for English diagonal and seventeenth-century cross-stitch.
7. ,,	.	.		T741–1899.	Neg. 44719.	
8. ,,	.	.		T8–1874.	Neg. 45474.	
9. Two samplers	.	.		T80–1925.	Neg. 55619.	Petit point.
10. Sampler	.	.	. On loan.	Neg. 55869.		Petit point sprays, figures, etc., and some counted designs.
11. ,,	.	.	. Worked by M. J.	T20–1913.		Powderings and fillings.
12. Chair-seat	.		. Neg. 57482.			Could be worked in petit point.
13. ,,	.		. Neg. 21769.			In Turkey knot ; could be worked in cross-stitch.
14. Fragment	.	.	. T50–1914.	,,	,,	,, ,,
15. Some bags	.		. Neg. 47616.			In petit point.
16. Carpet	.	.	. Neg. 54499.			All-over pattern in Turkey knot.
17. ,,	.	.	. Neg. 49200.			Powderings in cross-stitch.

These photographs and many others can be seen at the bookstall at the Victoria and Albert Museum, and can be ordered by post from the Secretary. They cost about 2s. each.

PLATE I.

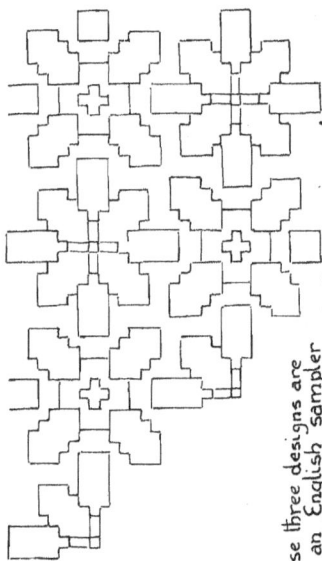

3.

These three designs are
on an English sampler
by M. C. date before 1640 in the possession of
Dr Glaisher.

4.

x represents
yellow in
this design.

5.

1. From a sampler dated 1657 belonging to
Sir William Lawrence. Bart.

Flowers shaded light to dark & dark to light alternately.

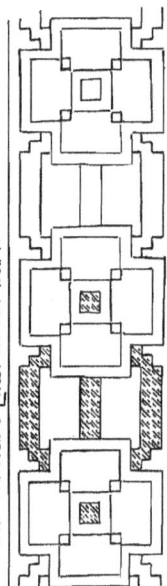

2. From a sampler
worked by M.J.
probably in 2nd quarter
of the 17th century.
T 20-1913. V.A.M.

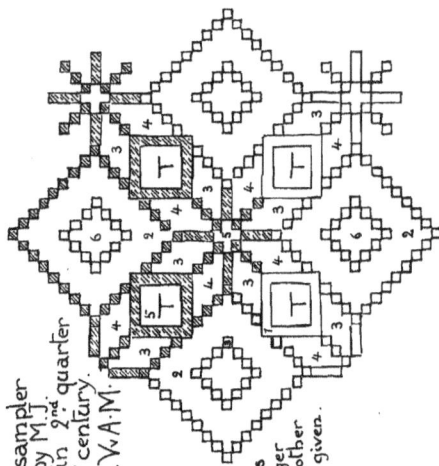

All outlines
are in nigger
unless another
colour is given.

1 nigger
2 green
3 red
4 blue
5 yellow
6 white

PLATE II.

Diagram from a fragment of a Stuart chair covering belonging to Aymas Phillips Esq worked in "crossed-corners" cross-stitch.

6

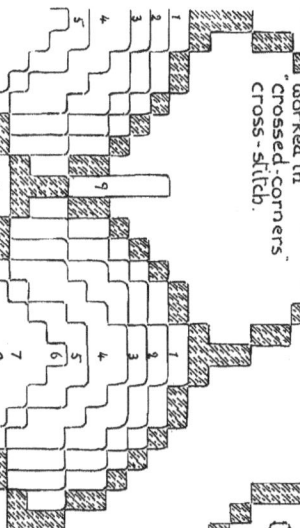

7

Suitable for the seat of a large chair if worked in crossed-corners

0 nigger   4 white
1 deep blue 5 pink
2 pale "   6 deep pink
3 middle " 7 rose red

8 From an old panel dated 1751. T59 - 1914 V·A·M

Outline nigger:
1 buff or beige
6 "   "
7 grey blue or green.
8 deeper than 7
9 dark grey blue or green.

The following vary in alternate diagonals
2 grey green or lemon yellow
3 blue or yellow green.
4 deeper blue or cinnamon
5 deepest - or brick red.

✗ represents a change of tone.
✗ represents the darkest colour in the design usually nigger.

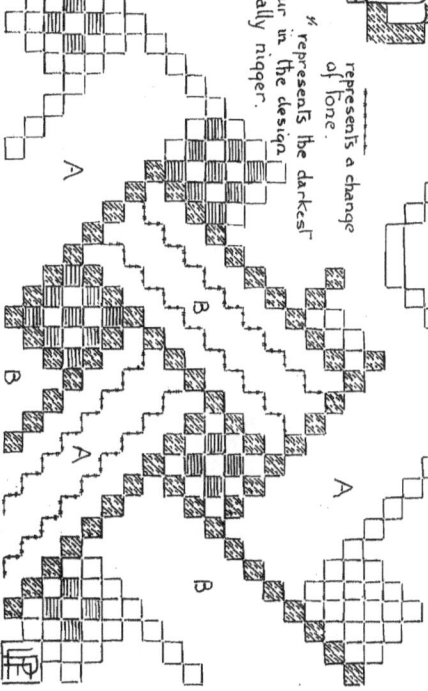

PLATE III.

11 Narrow border used to divide two of more importance. Such subsidiary borders are often kept to black, white or camel and are of much value to add emphasis to the whole design.

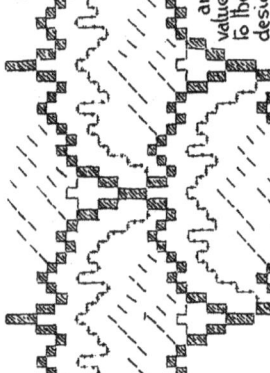

10

Scale design suitable for a chair. Outline cross-stitch filling in petit-point.

9

Simple form of scale design suitable for a beginner.

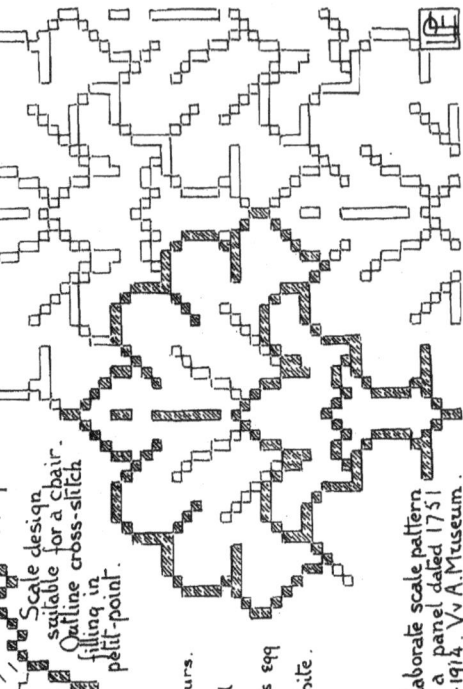

12 On an English sampler worked by M.C. prior to 1640 now owned by Dr Glaisber.

Original colours.
1 nigger
2 brick red
3 rose "
4 sparrow's egg
5 yellow
6 toned white.

13 An elaborate scale pattern from a panel dated 1751 T.59.1914. V. A. Museum.

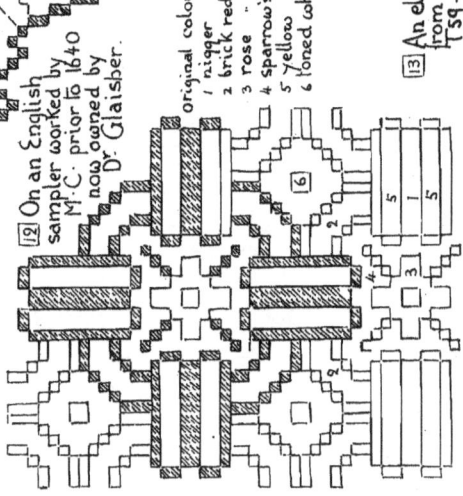

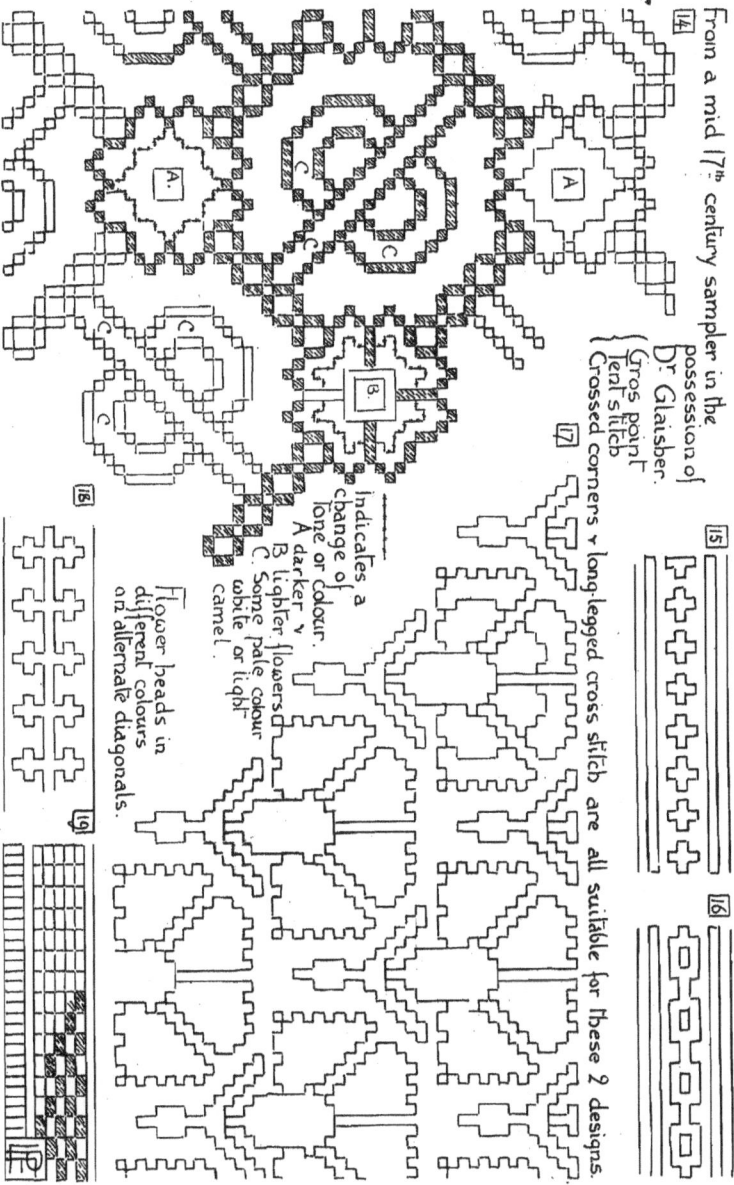

From a mid 17ᵗʰ century sampler in the possession of Dr Glaisher.

Gros point
Tent stitch
Crossed corners v long-legged cross stitch are all suitable for these 2 designs.

⌐ indicates a change of tone or colour.
A darker v
B lighter flowers
C. Some pale colour white or light camel.

Flower heads in different colours on alternate diagonals.

A.

A

B

C

14 15 16 17 18 19 20

PLATE IV.

PLATE V.

Suitable for carpet on a coarse canvas. Long-legged cross-stitch could be used lengthwise on each petal of the carnations

23 English sampler. 1st half of 17th Century. 1800-1918 V & A.M.

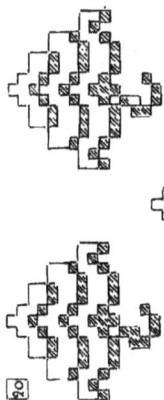

Nos 20, 21, 22 are from an old sampler worked in wools now in the possession of Miss Beddington.

The colour might vary on alternate diagonals or on alternate horizontal or vertical lines.

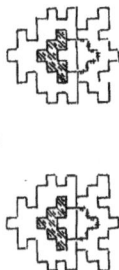

20

21

22

24

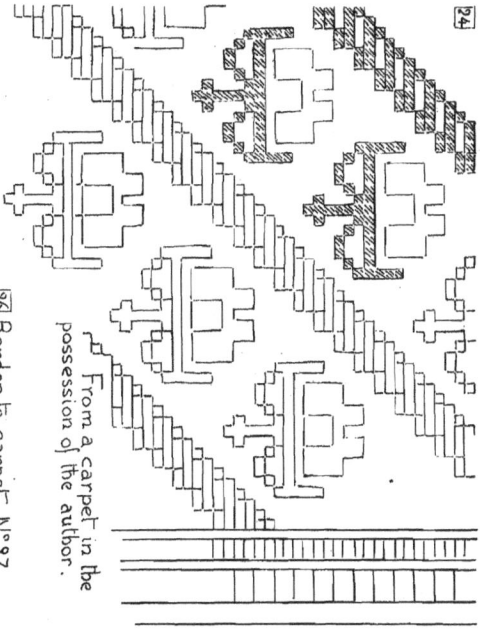

From a carpet in the possession of the author.

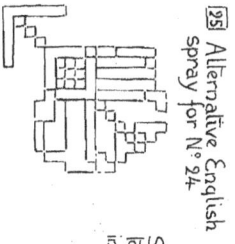

25 Alternative English spray for Nº 24.

26 Border to carpet Nº 27.

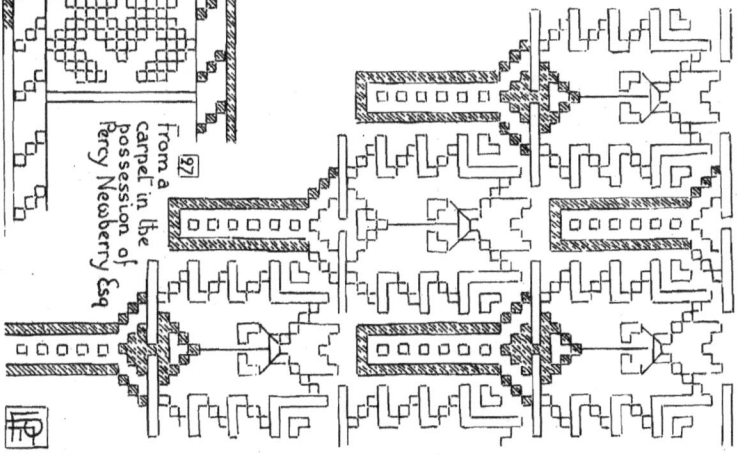

Skeleton to show interlacing

27 from a carpet in the possession of Percy Newberry Esq

PLATE VI.

PLATE VII.

This design with slight modifications occurs on eight or ten samplers examined by the author and can be seen in its different renderings in the Victoria and Albert Museum.

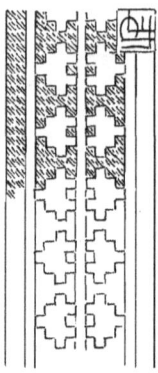

Types of border that are found on many of the old carpets and are useful as edgings for bags, cushions & covers.

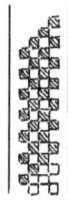

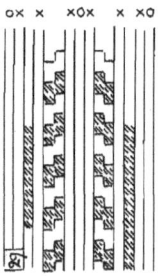

PLATE VIII.

From an English chair middle of 17th century

33

W 30-1923 Victoria v Albert Museum

worked in "Turkey knot".

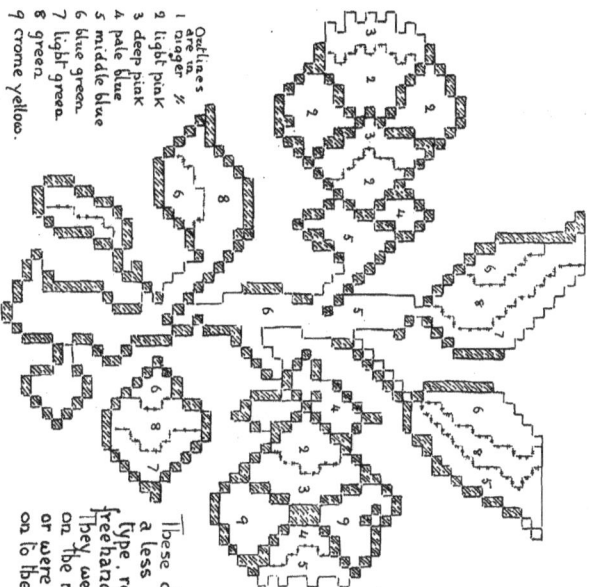

Outlines
are in
1 tinger %
2 light pink
3 deep pink
4 pale blue
5 middle blue
6 blue green
7 light green.
8 green.
9 crome yellow.

34

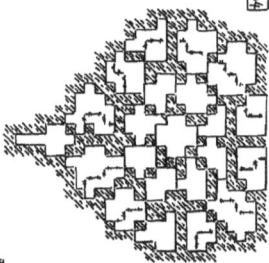

From a fragment in
Turkey knot
[T 50-1914 V. A.M]
These would be equally
suitable for cross-stitch
or petit-point the latter
gives a smaller scale.

35

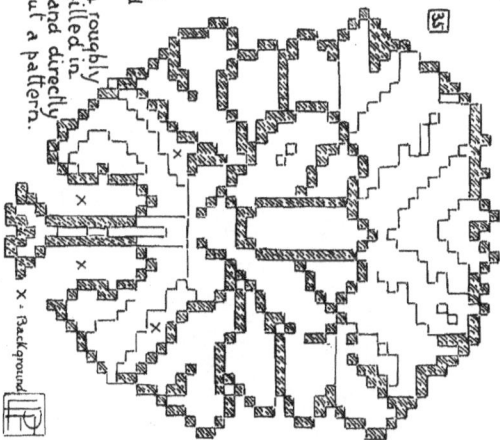

These designs are of
a less exact v formal
type. really a squared
freehand.
They were either drawn roughly
on the material v then filled in.
or were worked in freehand directly
on to the material without a pattern.

X = Background

PLATE IX.

36 From an English 17th sampler belonging to J. Jacoby Esq

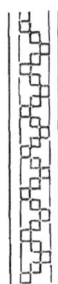

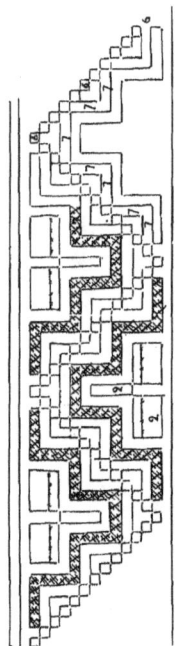

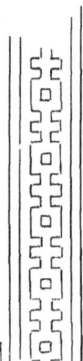

37

38

39

40

41

1 white
2 green <<<
3 red ////
4 pink
5 pale blue
6 middle blue
7 lemon yellow
8 orange

43

Sprays from a French sampler worked by Anne Mazelan v dated 1745. now in the possession of Mrs Longman.

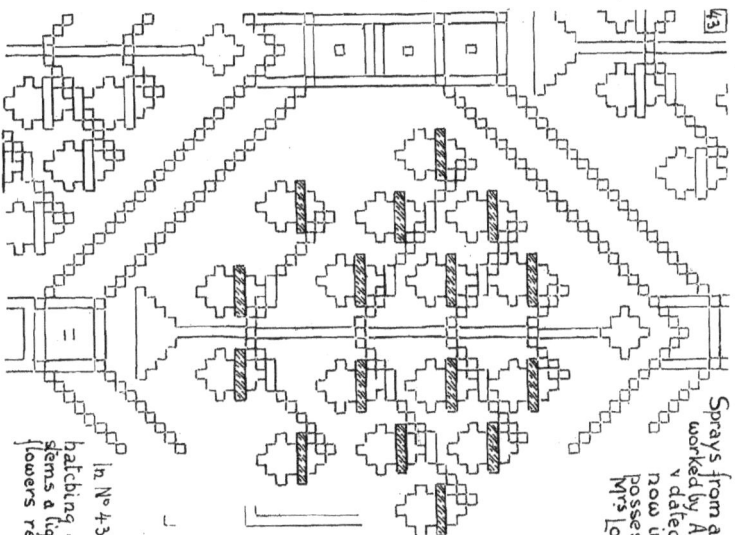

In Nº 43 hatching = blue green. stems a lighter green. flowers red.

44

A frame work has been added to these sprays as a suggestion for their use as details on a needlework carpet or rug v the main lines should be in nigger or black.

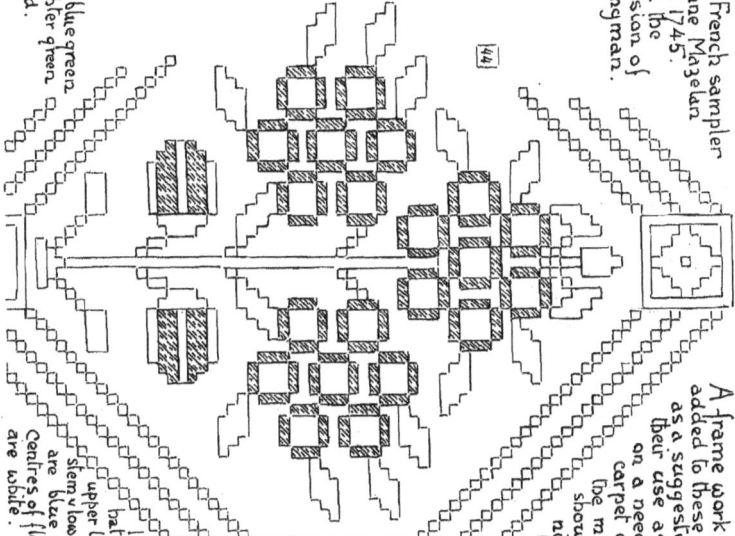

In Nº 44 hatching = red. upper leaves green. stem v lower leaves are blue green. Centres of flowers are white.

PLATE X.

www.ingramcontent.com/pod-product-compliance
Lightning Source LLC
Chambersburg PA
CBHW031221090426
42740CB00009B/1257